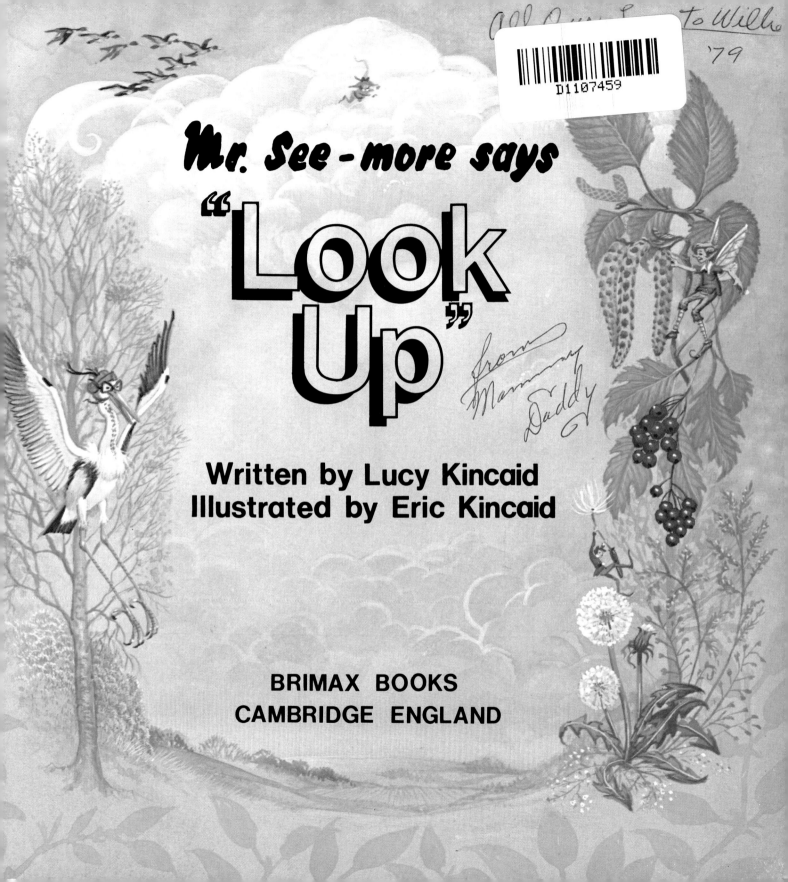

Mr. See-more says "Look Up"

Written by Lucy Kincaid
Illustrated by Eric Kincaid

BRIMAX BOOKS
CAMBRIDGE ENGLAND

Birds carry things

A bird has no pockets. A bird has no hands.
A bird carries things with its beak.

Feet positions

A bird's feet are like an undercarriage. It tucks them up when flying, and lowers them when landing.

Catkins

Catkins are not fairy socks pegged out to dry.

They grow on the tree. They are really flowers.

Fir cones

closed   open   seed

Cones open and close like suitcases. They keep
the tree seeds in order until the day they leave home.

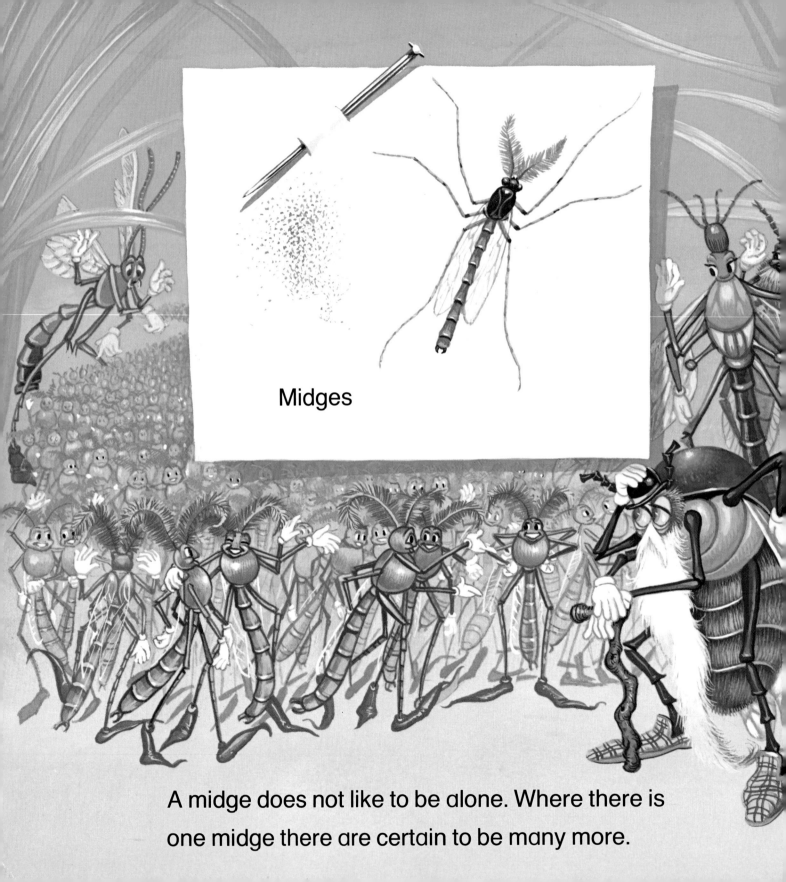

Midges

A midge does not like to be alone. Where there is one midge there are certain to be many more.

Flying insects

It is hard to tell what a small flying thing is.
Watch it until it lands and you might discover its identity.

Raindrops

Rain always falls in drips and drops. If it fell
in one piece everything would get squashed.

Snowflakes

Snow always falls in flakes. When it gets warm
it melts. There is no such thing as a warm snowflake.

Dandelion

A dandelion seed is like a parachute. It drifts
in the wind, and only the wind can make it hurry.

Nests

It is hard to tell when looking up at a nest whether it is empty or full.

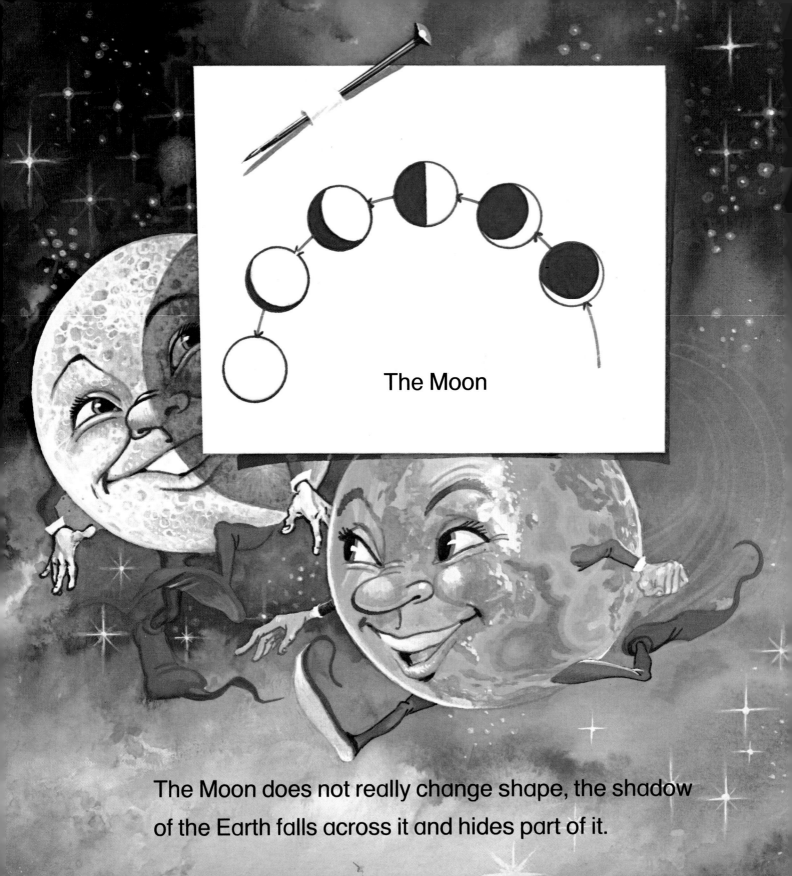

The Moon

The Moon does not really change shape, the shadow of the Earth falls across it and hides part of it.

Stars

The stars are far, far away. They shine all day
and all night, but we can only see them when it is dark.

Owl

Swallow

Blackbird

Crow

Silhouettes

Each bird has its own silhouette. There is no mistaking an owl for a swallow, or a blackbird for a crow.

Flying ducks

Ducks do not need flying lessons. They were flying in formation before aircraft were invented.

Leaf shapes

The shape of a leaf tells us from which tree it came.

A leaf *never* grows on the wrong tree.

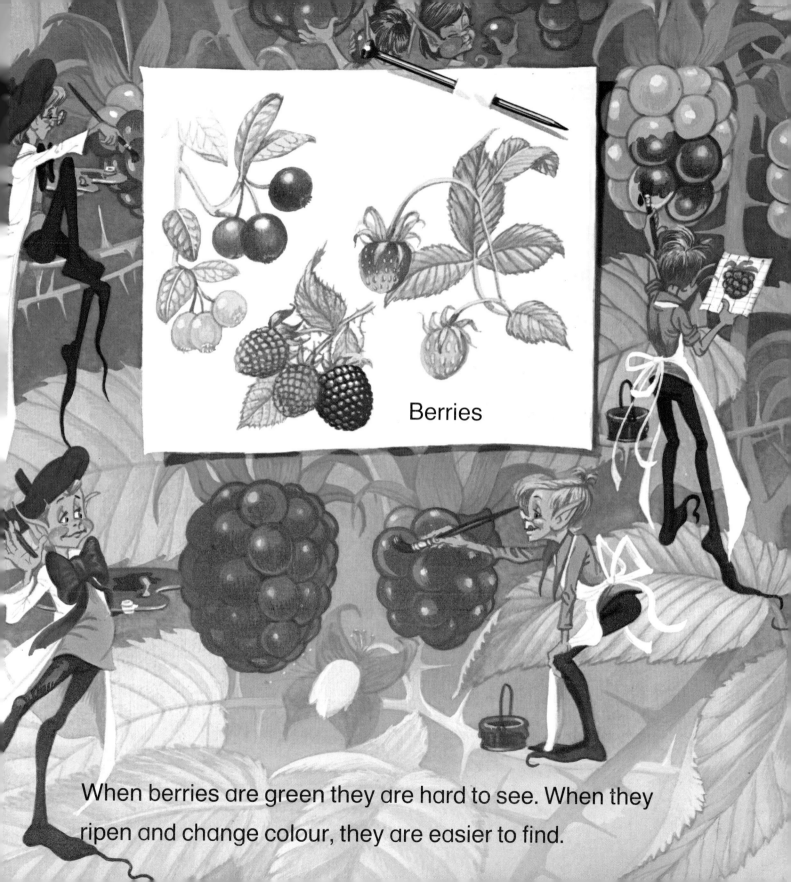

Berries

When berries are green they are hard to see. When they ripen and change colour, they are easier to find.

Squirrel

If a squirrel sees you before you see him, he will hide,
and then you will never know he was there at all.

Fledglings

Birds feed their babies until they are almost as big as themselves. Fledglings are always hungry.

Clouds

Clouds are very fidgety. They cannot keep still.

They are forever moving and changing shape.